# Book of Dinosaurs and Other Prehistoric Animals

An Educational Coloring Book

# NATIONAL WILDLIFE FEDERATION ®
# Book of Dinosaurs and Other
# Prehistoric Animals

Written by Beth Lyons
Cover and Interior Illustrations by Ken Maestas

Published in the United States of America by
EARTHBOOKS, INCORPORATED
7000 North Broadway, Suite 103
Denver, Colorado 80221
Steven W. Schmidt, President

Book of Dinosaurs and Other Prehistoric Animals
© 1991 EARTHBOOKS, INCORPORATED

ISBN 1-877731-16-1

Printed in Boulder, Colorado, USA

National Wildlife Federation®
©National Wildlife Federation
Licensed by Applause Licensing

# TABLE OF CONTENTS

# HOW TO USE THIS BOOK

This book begins with some general information about dinosaurs, prehistoric animals, and the people who first discovered them. Two time scales, one about animal and plant life many centuries ago and the other about the time each dinosaur was on Earth, are on pages 17 through 19. These will help you see which animals came before others in the history of these creatures. The dinosaurs and prehistoric animals in this book are arranged by the time line that begins on page 18. So, because Eryops is the oldest animal in this book, it is the first one for you to read about and color.

On all of the pages about each dinosaur you will see a picture of the dinosaur and a picture of a person. The person represents someone who is about six feet tall. When a person six feet tall stands next to the dinosaur you can get an idea of how big the dinosaur was. In some pictures the person seems very big next to the animal, and in others the dinosaur seems very big compared to the person.

Also these pages have maps of the places the dinosaurs lived. Although the Earth didn't look a lot like it does now, there were certain big parts of land that eventually became the continents. When you look at these maps and see a continent that is darkened, you will know that the animal on that page lived on that land mass- sometime before it really became the continent we know it as today.

When you begin coloring the creatures in this book, remember that no one truly knows what color dinosaurs and prehistoric animals were. You can color them any color you would like to use!

# WHAT IS A DINOSAUR?

A dinosaur is a prehistoric reptile that lived on land. Some scientists believe its closest relative may be crocodiles or birds. Some dinosaurs were small-about the size of a turkey. Others were huge-longer than two school buses and taller than a four-story building. And they came in all shapes and sizes and colors.

Scientists know about dinosaur shapes and sizes. They study dinosaur bones, or fossils, that have been dug from the ground. These bones are often buried in rock that was once thick, gooey mud or sand. Scientists don't know what colors the prehistoric animals were, though. But they can look at animals that live now and make good guesses.

### What is not a dinosaur?

Dinosaurs lived only on land and they lived only during the Age of Dinosaurs. So reptiles that flew were not dinosaurs. Reptiles that lived in the ocean also were not dinosaurs. The amphibians (animals that lived in the water and on land) were not dinosaurs. They lived before the dinosaurs were on Earth.

There also were mammal-like reptiles long ago. One had a huge sail-like fin on its back. It was big and fierce, but it was not a dinosaur, either. The mammal-like reptiles were here before the dinosaurs.

### What's in a name?

Some dinosaur names are pretty long. Maybe the words look too long to say. But there's a guide on each dinosaur page to help you. The dinosaur's name is followed by a key that shows how to say it. So go slow. And try the name out a few times. Before long, you'll be saying "Pachycephalosaurus" just like your own name.

Maybe you'll also want to give some of these animals a shorter nickname. You might choose the name "Packy" for Pachycephalosaurus. Or how about "Dippy" for Diprotodon? Or perhaps "Icky" for Ichthyosaurus? Anyway, have fun with them. They were pretty interesting creatures!

# WHAT HAPPENED TO THE DINOSAURS?

There were many dinosaurs living during the Age of Dinosaurs. This age is divided into three periods:

- **Triassic** (try-ASS-ik)
- **Jurassic** (joo-RASS-ik)
- **Cretaceous** (kreh-TAY-shus)

At the end of the last period, the Cretaceous Period (65 million years ago), all of the dinosaurs died. There were no survivors. Some scientists think they died at the same time all over the world—maybe in a single year. Others think they died over longer periods of time. But no one knows for sure—and the dinosaurs certainly didn't keep written records. So scientists have had to make some guesses. Here are a few of their ideas:

**1. The temperature got hotter.** In some areas of the Earth, the temperature changed during part of the Cretaceous Period. Everything became hotter—the air and the water. Perhaps the big dinosaurs got too hot. Some kinds of plants died, too. This left the dinosaurs with nothing to eat.

**2. The temperature got colder.** In the late Cretaceous Period, the temperature of the Earth may have been too cold for dinosaurs. They had no fur or feathers and most were too big to dig burrows. Some mammals and birds <u>did</u> survive because of their coverings. This cold temperature would have killed plants, too. Plants that were used to warm weather could not adapt. Then plant-eating dinosaurs were without food. When these dinosaurs died, the meat eaters were without food, too.

**3. The Earth's surface changed.** The dinosaurs died at the same time that huge mountain ranges were being formed (Rockies, Andes, Himalayas, Alps). This was also a time that large bodies of water became smaller. Swampy lands became dry. There were also many volcanoes then. Volcano ash may have destroyed the ozone layer. This would have let too much of the sun's deadly radiation reach the Earth.

**4. A nearby star exploded.** Sometimes when stars get very old, they explode. This gives off a lot of radiation. All that radiation would have caused temperatures to fall. This would have killed sea life. The shells of the eggs of the dinosaurs would not have protected the growing baby dinosaurs from the radiation and the eggs would not have hatched. It's also possible that the dinosaurs died from radiation at the time of the explosion.

**5. A killer asteroid hit the Earth.** This is the most popular idea. Scientists think that an asteroid, or small planet, smacked into Earth at the end of the Cretaceous Period. It hit with a force equal to 70 million big bombs. This asteroid may have been six miles wide and weighed four million tons. It would have formed a huge crater (bowl-shaped hole). This would then have sent rock and dust into the air.

This dust cloud would have drifted all over the Earth. It may have stayed for months or years. And it probably blocked the light from the sun. This would have killed plants, which would have killed plant-eating dinosaurs, which would have killed meat-eating dinosaurs. Get the picture?

There might have been other deadly effects of this asteroid:
- acid rain
- tidal waves (huge ocean waves that sometimes follow an earthquake)
- dark, freezing weather

- global warming and rising seas
- forest fires all over the world

So far, no crater has been found that is large enough or from the right time to support this idea. But scientists have found rocks with iridium in them. Iridium is a metal. It is very rare on Earth. But it is found in asteroids and comets. The iridium in these rocks just happens to be about 65 million years old.

Do you have any ideas about why the dinosaurs died? Maybe someday you'll be the person to make the big discovery.

# THE EARLY FOSSIL HUNTERS

Until about 150 years ago, no one knew that dinosaurs had ever lived. People thought the Earth had always been the same since time began. So when people came across fossils, they just didn't know what to think.

### Robert Plot

In 1677, Robert Plot wrote about a huge bone he had found in England. He even drew a picture of it. But he had no idea what it was. Was it a stone? Or part of an elephant? Or was it a bone from a huge man or woman? Plot didn't even think about prehistoric animals, though. No one thought about such things.

### Mary Ann Mantell

Many years later in England, Mary Ann Mantell found a huge fossil tooth in a pile of rocks. She showed it to her husband, Gideon, who collected fossils. He later found more teeth and bones in the same place. He thought the teeth looked like those of the present-day iguana, a lizard. But the fossil teeth were a whole lot bigger. Mantell decided to name his animal "Iguanodon."

### William Buckland

The first dinosaur that got a real scientific name was Megalosaurus, or "giant reptile." It was named by William Buckland in 1824. Bones of this animal had been found in a stone quarry.

### Sir Richard Owen

It was Richard Owen of England who first came up with the name "dinosaur." He knew that Iguanodon and Megalosaurus weren't just big reptiles. They were BIG, VERY OLD, EXTINCT reptiles. And he knew these bones were going to be very important one day.

## Mary Anning

One famous fossil hunter was only 10 years old. Mary Anning lived in England in the late 1800s. Her father got her interested in fossils. She found the first ichthyosaur fossils. An ichthyosaur (IK-thee-uh-sawr) was a fish-reptile and looked like a dolphin, only it had teeth. It lived in the sea during the dinosaur time. Mary also found the first pterodactyl (TAIR-uh-DAK-tuhl) fossil. This animal was a flying reptile. Some were the size of a crow; others were as large as small airplanes of today.

## Othniel Marsh and Edward Cope

England wasn't the only place where fossil hunting and naming were going on. There was a "bone war" or "dinosaur war" going on in America. Two paleontologists got a little carried away, though. A paleontologist (PAY-lee-on-TOL-uh-jist) is a person who studies the past using plant and animal fossils. The two men were Othniel Marsh and Edward Cope. They were bitter rivals. Each wanted to find the biggest and best dinosaur bones. And they refused to work together.

This "dinosaur war" was a good deal for science, though. At one time, only nine dinosaur species from North America were known. Then the teams of bone collectors went to work. Marsh's team found 80 new species. Cope's team found 56. This was a total of 136 new species.

Since that time, many more fossils have been found. People always seem to be interested in dinosaurs and other prehistoric animals. So maybe paleontology isn't such a dead subject after all!

# TIME SCALE

| Period | How Many Years Ago Began: | Animal and Plant Life |
|---|---|---|
| Quaternary | 2 million | Ancestors of people first appeared; most plants we have today |
| Tertiary | 65 million | Mammals, such as early elephants, camels, horses; many flowering plants and herb plants |
| Cretaceous | 136 million | New kinds of dinosaurs-duck-bill and armored, also lizards, small mammals; hardwood trees (oak, maple), flowering trees (dogwood), giant sequoias; roses and lilies |
| Jurassic | 190 million | Very large plant-eating dinosaurs, big meat-eating dinosaurs, small mammals; first birds; pine and palm trees, ginko trees; many kinds of fern plants |
| Triassic | 225 million | Early dinosaurs, flesh-eating reptiles, flying reptiles, small mammals (rodents); conifers, ginko trees; |
| Permian | 280 million | Amphibians, reptiles, mammal–like reptiles; many conifers (cone- bearing trees and shrubs) |
| Carboniferous | 345 million | Development of amphibians leading to reptiles; insects; giant ferns, first conifers |
| Devonian | 395 million | First insects, beetles cockroaches; Age of Fish; first amphibians; ferns, some land plants |

# Time Scale of Dinosaurs and Prehistoric Animals

| | | • Apatosaurus |
|---|---|---|
| | • Cynognathus | • Ichthyosaurus |
| | • Lystrosaurus | • Archaeopteryx |
| | • Tanystropheus | • Brachiosaurus |
| | • Thecodontosaurus | • Compsognathus |
| • Eryops | • Staurikosaurus | • Rhamphorhynchus |

Permian Period

Triassic Period

Jurassic Period

280 million
years ago

225 million
years ago

190 million
years ago

|  |  |  |
| --- | --- | --- |
| • Iguanodon | • Alticamelus | • Diprotodon |
| • Psittacosaurus | • Baluchitherium | • Glyptodon |
| • Pachycephalosaurus | • Diatryma | • Megatherium |
|  | • Platybelodon |  |

Cretaceous Period    Tertiary Period    Quaternary Period

**136 million
years ago**

**65 million
years ago**

**2 million
years ago**

# ERYOPS
## Permian Period

**Eryops** (AIR-ee-ops)

Does Eryops remind you of any swamp animal of today–maybe an alligator or a crocodile? Eryops does look similar to these. But Eryops was an amphibian (am-FIB-ee-uhn). Alligators and crocodiles are reptiles.

What's the difference between an amphibian and a reptile? For one thing, an amphibian has moist, smooth skin. A typical reptile has dry, scaly skin. Another difference is where these animals lay their eggs. An amphibian, which can live on land or in the water, lays its eggs near or in water. This is the only place the eggs can survive. A reptile, however, lays its eggs on land. These eggs have a tough shell. They hold moisture so the inside doesn't dry out.

Eryops, an amphibian, came after fish but before reptiles and mammals. Amphibians evolved (developed slowly) from fish. Little by little the fish grew legs where its fins had been. Then it was able to walk on land and swim in water.

During Eryops's time, there were no dinosaurs yet, nor were there any birds. But there were many kinds of fish. Early reptiles were also starting to appear. And it was still hot and steamy, so the land was covered with creeping ferns, tough new plants, and tall trees.

Eryops spent much of its life on land, even though it was an amphibian. It had to look for food—mainly small land animals. It was a fierce hunter with sharp teeth in its huge mouth. It didn't really use those teeth for chewing, though. It used them for grabbing live food and tearing it into smaller pieces. Then it gulped down the food whole or in chunks. Even the name Eryops refers to its snout. The name means "drawn-out face." And it did have a rather long snout.

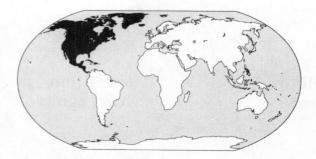

# CYNOGNATHUS
## Early to Middle Triassic Period

**Cynognathus** (sy-noh-NAY-thus)

You know about reptiles that lived in prehistoric times. These included small reptiles as well as huge dinosaurs. And there were mammals back then, too. To confuse things even more, there also were mammal-like reptiles. Cynognathus was one of these.

As we zoom back in time, we visit the Cynognathus family on a hot summer day. Actually, most days all year are hot. In this Triassic Period, there is little rain and no snow. Much of the land is dry like a desert. There are some green plants growing near ponds, but there are no grasses or flowers yet.

Earlier in the day, an adult Cynognathus chased and killed a plant-eating animal. This is no big deal for Cynognathus because it is a fast runner. It also has sharp front teeth and long killer canine teeth. The adult takes its prey back to the den. It has young ones to feed. When the young were first born, they fed on their mother's milk. They did not have a full set of teeth for chewing meat. But now that they are older, they eat meat like the adults.

This scene is somewhat like a wolf family of today. In fact, Cynognathus may have looked like a large wolf with a big head. It was probably hairy like a mammal and had mammal-like teeth. So why is it called a mammal-like reptile?

The main answer is in the jaw. Cynognathus had a jaw like a reptile. It was a primitive, or early, kind of jaw. It had bones that mammals don't have. And Cynognathus probably couldn't hear well because it had primitive ears, too. Scientists aren't sure about the babies of mammal-like reptiles. Were they born alive or did they hatch from eggs? There also is no sure way to tell if Cynognathus was warm-blooded or cold-blooded. Scientists tend to think it was warm-blooded because the animal had a coat of hair.

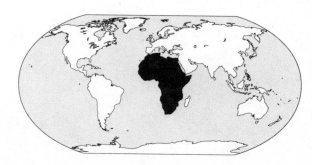

23

# LYSTROSAURUS
## Early Triassic Period

**Lystrosaurus** (list-roh-SAWR-us)

Antarctica is a cold, frozen land. It is covered by a huge sheet of ice even in the summer. Scientists do research in Antarctica, but few people live there year-round. Because it is so cold, it is not the most popular place for fossil hunting. Lystrosaurus is one of the few prehistoric animals ever found there.

Bones of Lystrosaurus have also been found in India and South Africa. Does this mean the animal lived on three different continents—Antarctica, Asia, and Africa? Scientists think that these continents were once joined together. The large land mass was called Pangea. Over millions of years, the land split up and became the seven continents we now know.

Antarctica must have been very different during the time of Lystrosaurus. There were rivers and lakes and swamps. Many land and water plants gave this animal plenty to eat. It was certainly much warmer then, too.

Lystrosaurus looked like a dog with a turtle's head. Although it was a reptile, it was like a mammal in some ways. Its body looked like that of a mammal. It also had sharp canine tusks, or teeth, like a dog. So Lystrosaurus was called a mammal-like reptile.

Lystrosaurus was different from the other mammal-like reptiles, though. It lived in water or on land like the hippopotamus of today. It looked clumsy on land. It was slow and waddled when it walked. But in the water it was a graceful swimmer. It could also stay underwater and watch for its enemies. That's because its eyes and nostrils were on top of its head.

The early Triassic Period was a time just before the dinosaurs came to be. The Earth was ruled by the mammal-like reptiles. These reptiles died out toward the end of the Triassic Period, though. The climate changed from hot and dry to warm and wet. There was much heavy rainfall. Swamps formed where deserts had been. Perhaps the mammal-like reptiles could not adapt to this new climate.

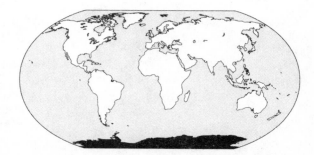

# TANYSTROPHEUS
## Middle Triassic Period

**Tanystropheus** (tan-iss-TROH-fee-us)

When the first bones of Tanystropheus were found, scientists were stumped. The bones were almost ten feet long. They were thought to be leg bones—but from whose legs? Then a full skeleton was found. It was discovered that these ten-foot bones were actually neck bones. Tanystropheus was a lizard with a neck that was longer than its body and tail <u>together</u>.

Tanystropheus may have spent much of its time in or near the water. Its ten-foot neck could search below the surface of the water for fish and small amphibians (am-FIB-ee-unz). Amphibians are animals that can live on land or in the water. Tanystropheus could probably poke its head into narrow rock openings to look for food.

This giant lizard was not a good swimmer, though. It had regular legs, not fins. It also had a fairly short, round tail, not a flat one. Its legs and tail could not propel it through the water.

Tanystropheus was not too swift on land, either. Notice its legs. They came out from the sides of the body, like most reptiles. These legs could not support the weight of the body very well. Therefore, Tanystropheus could not run very fast. This is different from some other animals, like the later dinosaurs and today's mammals. Their legs are straight below the body. These legs can support the body, especially for animals that weigh a ton.

Like other creatures that ate fish, Tanystropheus had needle-sharp teeth. These teeth helped it spear and hold onto fish. This was important so the fish couldn't squirm away once it was caught. Tanystropheus clamped its jaws tight until the fish was surely dead. Then it swallowed the fish whole. It had only these sharp teeth and no flat teeth for grinding and chewing.

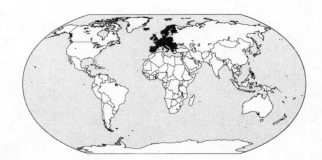

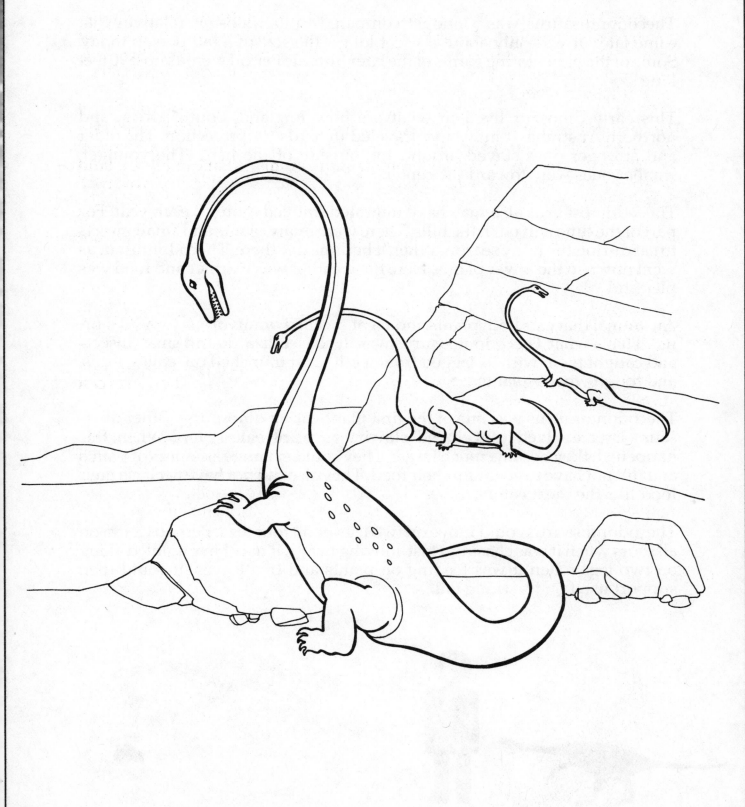

# THECODONTOSAURUS
## Triassic Period

**Thecodontosaurus** (THEE-koh-DON-tuh-SAWR-us)

Thecodontosaurus was a midget compared to its dinosaur relatives that came later. It was only about six feet long—the size of a tall person today. Some of the plant-eating giants of the later Jurassic Period were almost 90 feet long.

This early dinosaur lived in what are now England, South Africa, and northern Australia. It may have traveled in herds for protection. The older and stronger ones stayed around the outside of the herd. The younger, smaller ones were toward the center.

Thecodontosaurus also may have migrated (moved around) each year. For part of the time it lived in the hills. There were many plants and small insects to eat during the rainy season. When it became dry there, Thecodontosaurus went down to the lower plains. Here the weather was warmer and food was plentiful.

An animal that eats both plants and meat is called omnivorous (om-NIV-or-us). That's what Thecodontosaurus was. It chased lizards and small insects and caught them with its jagged front teeth. Or it munched on leaves, ferns, and tough woody plants.

Thecodontosaurus was one of the first plant-eating dinosaurs. Other dinosaurs later evolved (developed slowly) as plant eaters, too. When this happened, they became much larger. They could eat huge amounts of plants and did not have to go far for their food. They also did not have to chase their food like the meat eaters.

Thecodontosaurus could move on two legs or on four legs. Perhaps it ran on all fours when it was chasing a fast-moving lizard. It may have ambled along on two legs when it was feeding on plants and tree leaves. It could then support itself on its strong tail.

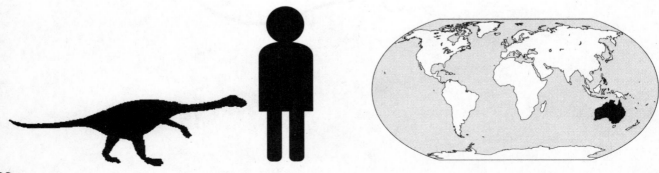

# STAURIKOSAURUS
## Late Triassic Period

**Staurikosaurus** (stawr-IK-uh-SAWR-us)

One of the earliest known dinosaurs was Staurikosaurus. It looked somewhat like a cross between a lizard and a giant chicken. It had a lightweight body and moved on two legs. This was a real advantage because it allowed the animal to run fast. It could often outrun its enemies and its prey.

Staurikosaurus was about six feet long. It had a big head compared to the size of its body. Don't let that fool you, though. The large head did not contain a large brain. But it did contain a large jaw with many sharp teeth. These teeth had a slight backward curve. This let the dinosaur get a good grip on its victim. Staurikosaurus probably ate the small mammals that lived then. They were like rats or mice of today.

Staurikosaurus had long hind legs with five toes. Its short arms had five fingers. These long fingers could grab and tear the flesh of small animals. Its long neck could reach out and snap at the many insects that flew around it.

Even though Staurikosaurus had a small brain, it was no dummy. It may have watched for the bigger meat eaters to make a kill. Staurikosaurus would wait until the bigger creature ate its fill. Then it would move in and clean up the leftovers.

The Earth during the time of Staurikosaurus was warm and dry. There were deserts, swamps, and huge forests. Many of the forests had pine trees and palm trees. There were very few big dinosaurs yet. But there were early crocodiles and flying reptiles. The small mammals that lived then tried to stay hidden from all their larger enemies, including Staurikosaurus.

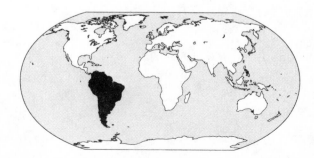

# APATOSAURUS
## Jurassic Period

**Apatosaurus** (uh-PAT-uh-SAWR-us)

In the late 1800s there was a "bone war" going on in this country. People had known about dinosaur fossils for quite a while. Two men, though, were real fossil nuts. They were Othniel Marsh and Edward Cope. Each wanted to find the biggest and best dinosaur bones. But they refused to work together. They were bitter rivals.

It was Marsh who found some bones of Apatosaurus in 1877. But the skeleton was not complete. He was unable to find the animal's skull. Marsh, however, was in a hurry to show off this huge new discovery. He couldn't leave it headless, though. So he gave it a skull that he claimed had been found near Apatosaurus. But it wasn't really an Apatosaurus head. And for many years people called this dinosaur by another name—Brontosaurus (BRON-tuh-SAWR-us).

It wasn't until 1979 that the real Apatosaurus head was found. And it wasn't square like a box as people had thought. It was quite long and thin and very small compared to the rest of the body. It also had a fairly small brain—maybe the smallest for its body weight of any animal with a backbone.

Apatosaurus was a giant among giants. It weighed more than 20 tons. It was about as long as two school buses put together. It also had a long, flexible neck, much like a giraffe of today. It could eat leaves from the tallest trees. It probably swallowed the leaves whole, though. It had no molars (flat back teeth) for grinding food.

Apatosaurus may have traveled in herds, like elephants do today. The adults stayed on the outside to protect the small young ones in the center of the group. Herds sometimes waded into deep water to escape enemies. They were probably able to float, too. They may have used their long tails as anchors.

# ICHTHYOSAURUS
## Middle to Late Jurassic Period

**Ichthyosaurus** (IK-thee-uh-SAWR-us)

During the Jurassic Period, certain animals ruled the land, the air, and the sea. Dinosaurs, of course, were the giants of the land. In the air flew the pterosaurs (TAIR-uh-sawrz). Some of them had wingspans as large as small airplanes of today. The seas were ruled by a fish-shaped reptile called Ichthyosaurus. Its name means "fish lizard."

Ichthyosaurus was not a fish, although it looked much like a shark of today. It had a huge tail fin that moved up and down. This propelled it through the water. The paddle–like fins were good for steering and moving through the water. Ichthyosaurus also had a fin on its back. This helped it steer and kept it steady in the water.

Sea reptiles like Ichthyosaurus could not leave the water to lay their eggs. They had no way to move on land. They overcame this problem, though. The females gave birth to live young, just as mammals do.

When it came time to find food, Ichthyosaurus had two advantages. First, it had huge eyes. It could spot fish at the bottom of a pond or between rocks. Second, it had many sharp teeth in its long, pointed snout. Squirmy fish were easily trapped and couldn't get away. Ichthyosaurus probably swallowed the fish whole. Its sharp teeth were for grabbing, not for chewing and grinding.

There were many large swamps and other bodies of water during the Jurassic Period. This was a time that the Earth was wet and warm. There was much rainfall. Huge plants grew in places that had once been deserts. There were also many trees, including evergreens and palms. There were no flowers or grasses yet, though. Those came later. The Jurassic Period was the perfect time for growing giants—both plants and animals.

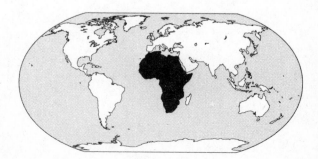

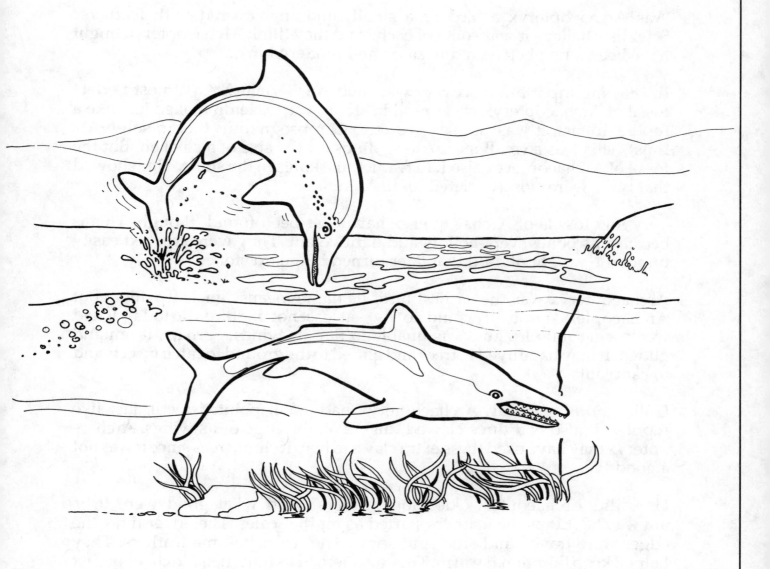

# ARCHAEOPTERYX
## Late Jurassic Period

**Archaeopteryx** (ARK-ee-OP-ter-iks)

Was Archaeopteryx a bird or a small dinosaur covered with feathers? Scientists believe it was some of each. And they think Archaeopteryx might have been a link between dinosaurs and modern birds.

In 1861 an important discovery was made in Germany. An almost perfect fossil of Archaeopteryx was found in stone. The skeleton looked just like a reptile. In fact, it was similar in size to Compsognathus (komp-soh-NAY-thus). This was a small meat-eating dinosaur the size of a chicken. But the fossil of Archaeopteryx also had feather markings in the stone. This showed that birds were closely related to dinosaurs.

Very few fossils of Archaeopteryx have ever been found, though. This is because its bones were hollow and lightweight. They were crushed easily under the weight of mud that later turned into hard stone.

Archaeopteryx was the earliest bird. Its name means "ancient wing." But Archaeopteryx probably could not fly—at least not like birds do today. It had weak wing muscles and was unable to flap its wings. Perhaps it ran and glided. It may have lived in trees and glided to the ground to catch insects and to eat plants.

Unlike birds of today, Archaeopteryx had small pointed teeth, just like reptiles. It also had three clawed fingers on the edge of its wings. Archaeopteryx may have used these extra claws to help it climb trees since it was not a good flier.

How did Archaeopteryx develop feathers? And what good were they, anyway? Perhaps the feathers started as reptile scales. Then over time, the edges were frayed and stuck out some. The scales became feathers. They helped keep the animal warm. They also served as huge nets. Archaeopteryx chased insects and small animals. It probably used its feathered arms to catch its prey.

# BRACHIOSAURUS
## Late Jurassic Period

**Brachiosaurus** (BRAK-ee-uh-SAWR-us)

Here's a dinosaur that didn't weigh a ton—it weighed 50 tons! Do you have any idea how much 50 tons is? That's like putting ten African elephants together—all in one animal. Brachiosaurus was one of the heaviest four-legged animals that ever lived.

With its neck stretched out, Brachiosaurus was about 40 feet tall. That's about as tall as a four-story building today. It could eat from the tallest trees. And did it ever eat! To fill up such a huge body, this dinosaur had to eat lots of plants. It was constantly eating leaves and pine needles and bits of twigs.

Like some other plant eaters, Brachiosaurus did not chew its food at all. It had teeth for snipping leaves but no teeth for chewing them. And some of its food, like pine needles, was tough and woody. So Brachiosaurus swallowed the leaves and needles and twigs whole.

Brachiosaurus was built like a giraffe but on a much larger scale. Its front legs were longer than its back legs. That's why it is called the "arm lizard." Its back sloped all the way from its shoulders to its hips. It breathed through nostrils (nose holes) on top of its head. This allowed it to chew and swallow food and breathe, all at the same time.

Because Brachiosaurus was so tall, it may have been a good lookout for other animals. Giraffes do this today. Smaller animals, like zebras, look for food near giraffes. Then when the giraffes spot danger in the distance, all the animals can run to safety.

Scientists think there may have been one or two other dinosaurs even larger than Brachiosaurus. Whole skeletons have not been found yet. It is believed, though, that they may have weighed almost 80 tons. For now, these mystery dinosaurs are just called "Supersaurus" and "Ultrasaurus."

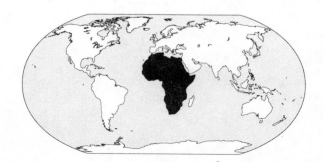

# COMPSOGNATHUS
## Late Jurassic Period

**Compsognathus** (komp-soh-NAY-thus)

How do you think one of the smallest dinosaurs was like one of the largest? Compsognathus was the tiniest carnivore (KAR-nuh-vohr), or meat eater. Tyrannosaurus (ty-RAN-uh-SAWR-us) was the largest meat eater. Also, these two dinosaurs had the same number of toes (three on each foot) and fingers (two on each hand). But they lived in different times and in different places. And their sizes were worlds apart, too. Compsognathus was about two feet long. Tyrannosaurus was about 50 feet long.

A very good fossil of Compsognathus was found in Germany. The bones were preserved in limestone. Near the animal's stomach were also found the bones of a lizard. This shows the kind of prey that Compsognathus went after. It probably also ate large and small insects and newly hatched baby dinosaurs. And if it came upon a dead fish or other dead animal, it happily ate that, too.

The name Compsognathus means "pretty jaw" or "graceful jaw." You can decide for yourself if you think the name fits. It also had long, skinny legs and short, skinny arms. Those skinny legs, though, were swift and powerful. This little dinosaur scurried on small dry islands, always searching for food—or trying to escape the bigger dinosaurs.

One of the strange things about Compsognathus was that it may have given birth to live young. This is something that is true of mammals but not of most reptiles. The dinosaurs laid eggs, as do most reptiles of today. Compsognathus may have been a different sort of dinosaur, though.

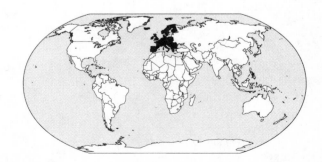

# RHAMPHORHYNCHUS
## Late Jurassic Period

**Rhamphorhynchus** (ram-for-RING-kus)

Rhamphorhynchus was birdlike but it was not a bird because it had no feathers. It also was not a dinosaur. It was a flying reptile. But unlike reptiles that are cold-blooded, this animal may have been warm-blooded. Bats, too, of today are warm-blooded. Warm-blooded means that the body temperature stays about the same all the time, no matter what the surroundings are like.

The name Rhamphorhynchus means "knife beak" or "beak nose." You can probably see why. It had a thin, pointed head with a long beak. Its sharp teeth slanted forward. These teeth helped it spear and hold fish in its mouth. Rhamphorhynchus could fly or glide just over the surface of the water. It had big eyes and could see very well. So it could spot a fish, swoop down, and then grab the fish with its long beak.

Rhamphorhynchus was a kind of pterosaur (TAIR-uh-sawr). These were winged lizards. They had wide, thin wings that stretched from the end of a fourth finger. Rhamphorhynchus had a wingspan of four feet. That's about the height of a small person. But some kinds of pterosaurs were huge. They had wingspans like small airplanes of today. Some pterosaurs could flap their wings. Others just glided on the warm air currents.

Even though Rhamphorhynchus had large wings, its body was not so big. It was only 18 inches long. And it had an odd tail. It was very stiff and had a flap of skin at the end. This flap was like a rudder. Maybe you've heard of a rudder on a boat. This helps the boat to steer. Well, this tail flap helped Rhamphorhynchus steer as it flew.

Few fossils of Rhamphorhynchus have been found. This is true of most pterosaurs. Some fossils were found in Africa and parts of Europe. But many of the creatures' bones were probably crushed. That's because their bones were hollow. This gave them lightweight bodies for flying. As a result, though, when these animals died, their bones were crushed by the weight of all kinds of rock except limestone.

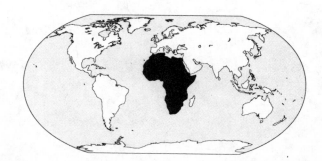

# IGUANODON
## Cretaceous Period

**Iguanodon** (ih-GWAH-nuh-don)

Iguanodon became famous almost overnight. Its tooth was one of the first dinosaur fossils ever found. This started a new excitement about these strange reptiles of long ago. Until that time, people knew almost nothing about dinosaurs.

In 1822, Mary Ann Mantell found the first Iguanodon tooth among some rocks. She gave it to her husband, who collected fossils. He thought it looked like the tooth of a present-day iguana, which is a small lizard. You might guess, then, that the name Iguanodon means "iguana tooth."

Iguanodon looked somewhat like a huge kangaroo covered with scales. It may have used its giant tail to beat off its enemies. And if it got tired, Iguanodon could lean back and sit on its tail. Scientists can tell from its tracks that Iguanodon was a fast runner at times. When it ran, it lifted its tail off the ground and bent forward. But at seven tons, it was hardly a track star.

Unlike the iguana, Iguanodon walked on its hind legs or all fours. Iguanodon had powerful hind legs with birdlike feet. These feet had three toes with claws at the end. The arms were much smaller than its legs. It also had hands somewhat like human hands, except for its spiked thumb. This thumb may have been used by males to attract females. Or it might have been used as a sharp weapon. Sometimes this thumb grew to be 16 inches long. That's quite a natural weapon!

Although Iguanodon looked fierce, it was not a killer. It ate only plants. So it was called an herbivore (URB-uh-vohr). It was 15 to 20 feet long, which is about as high as a two-story house. Iguanodon could eat leaves from the upper branches of many trees. It used its hands to grab and hold branches while it ate.

Iguanodon lived during the Cretaceous Period. This was the Age of Dinosaurs. There were more dinosaurs living at this time than ever before. But at the end of this period, almost all of the dinosaurs died out.

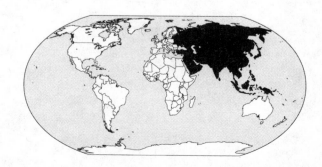

# PSITTACOSAURUS
## Early Cretaceous Period

**Psittacosaurus** (sih-TAK-uh-SAWR-us)

Psittacosaurus was much smaller than some of the other dinosaurs of its time. It was only about six feet tall. Some babies of Psittacosaurus that have been found were only ten inches long—less than the length of a ruler.

The name Psittacosaurus means "parrot lizard." This is a good name for it because it had a beak like a parrot. The beak looks like a strange overbite. It probably helped Psittacosaurus eat plants.

This dinosaur ate other things as well. Actually, it probably ate parts of trees and may have even tried pine cones. For that kind of diet, Psittacosaurus needed very strong jaws and sharp teeth. The hooked beak bit off leaves, stems, and twigs. Then the back teeth worked like a pair of scissors. They chopped up the food and churned it around. With these teeth and the powerful jaw muscles, says one scientist, Psittacosaurus could have eaten wooden boards.

It is believed that Psittacosaurus walked upright on its hind legs. Fossils show that the hind legs were long and the front arms were short. Also, Psittacosaurus came <u>after</u> the early plant eaters that walked on two legs. But it was <u>before</u> the late plant eaters that walked on four legs.

It looks like Psittacosaurus also had its own kind of armor. Notice that it had a neck shield right at the end of its head. This was a piece of solid bone. It was probably there for protection from enemies. Some fossils of shields do show teeth marks. Psittacosaurus did not have horns. But it is believed that it was an early ancestor of the dinosaurs that did have huge horns and thick neck shields.

Other reptiles that lived during the time of Psittacosaurus included the giant Iguanodon and smaller plant eaters. Tortoises and crocodiles lived at that time, too.

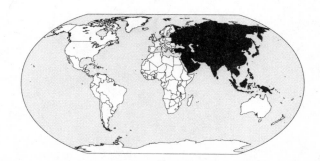

# PACHYCEPHALOSAURUS
## Late Cretaceous Period

**Pachycephalosaurus** (pak-ee-SEF-uh-loh-SAWR-us)

Pachycephalosaurus was a real bonehead. It had a thick bony dome on top of its head. This dome sometimes grew as thick as ten inches. That's thicker than your whole head.

The name Pachycephalosaurus means "thick head." Scientists aren't really even sure what this thick dome was for. Maybe the dinosaur used its bonehead for fighting. Two of them may have butted heads to show which one was superior. Rams and bighorn sheep of today do that. Perhaps these dinosaurs ran at each other full speed and slammed into each other's heads. So it was a good thing that these domes were like football helmets. But then, this butting couldn't have hurt their brains too much. They were only about the size of a walnut.

Besides the thick dome, Pachycephalosaurus also had spikes and big warts on its face. The spikes may have been used to dig up plants. And the face may have been ugly enough to scare its enemies away.

There were different kinds of boneheads in the time that Pachycephalosaurus lived. These boneheads came in different sizes—small, medium, and large. The smaller ones were about the size of a turkey. The medium ones were about as big as a large person. The largest ones were about 20 feet long, or the length of a living room.

This dinosaur may have been related to the duckbill dinosaurs. It had a mouth that was somewhat flat like a duck's bill. There were many sharp teeth in its mouth for eating tough water plants and land plants. And there were many plants on Earth during the Cretaceous Period. This was toward the end of the Age of Dinosaurs. By then, flowering plants were everywhere. Many of these, like the rose, still exist. But Pachycephalosaurus, of course, is long gone.

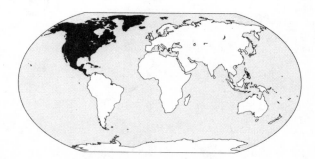

# ALTICAMELUS
## Tertiary Period

**Alticamelus** (al-tee-KAM-uh-lus)

This early mammal lived in North America about 20 million years ago. It was a camel that really looked more like a giraffe. The name Alticamelus means "high camel." And its head <u>was</u> pretty high off the ground—10 to 15 feet. At that height, it could eat leaves from the tops of trees.

Alticamelus was not like the camels of the desert today. It had no hump for storing food. Its neck was longer than a camel's, too. And Alticamelus lived on the open plains near wooded areas, rather than on hot, dry deserts. Because it was more like a giraffe than a camel, it is sometimes called a giraffe-camel.

This giraffe-camel was not an ancestor of the modern camel, though. It was part of the camel family, but then it died out. It left no descendants (those who came after). The true ancestor of the camel may have been an animal that looks like the llama of South America.

Alticamelus was a pretty gawky-looking creature. It had skinny, spindly legs with knobby knees. It looked as if it were standing on stilts. And it probably looked like easy prey to some of the meat-eating animals of that time. Wolflike creatures prowled the grasslands. They crept through the tall grass, waiting for the right moment to attack any animals in the open.

It was lucky that Alticamelus had a secret weapon, though. Those spindly legs had sharp, pointed toes. Alticamelus could rear up on its back legs. Then it could smack its enemy with its front feet. This not only caught the wolf off guard, it may also have smashed its head or chest. Then Alticamelus could gallop away to safety.

Alticamelus lived during the Age of Mammals, after the big dinosaurs had died out. Like most other mammals, it had hair on its body to keep it warm. The Earth at that time was colder than it had been during the dinosaur age.

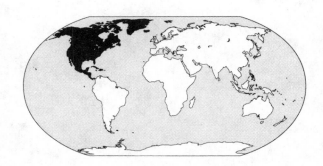

50

# BALUCHITHERIUM
Tertiary Period

**Baluchitherium** (buh-LOO-chuh-THEE-ree-um)

The rhinoceros of today is a midget compared with some of its ancestors. Baluchitherium was an early rhino that lived in Asia. Its name means "the beast from Baluchistan." Baluchistan is a region in western Pakistan in Asia. This is where the fossil of this animal was first found.

Baluchitherium was big—VERY BIG. Just how big was it? Well, a human adult would be able to look it right in the knee. (Remember, though, that there were no humans living at the time of Baluchitherium.) This animal could easily eat leaves and twigs from the tops of the tallest trees. Baluchitherium was also pretty hefty. It weighed about 20 tons. That's more than twice as much as an elephant weighs. Still, at 20 tons, it weighed less than half of what the largest dinosaur weighed!

Baluchitherium was a mammal, not a dinosaur. The dinosaur was a reptile. There's a difference between a mammal and a reptile. A mammal feeds its young on the mother's milk. It also has hair and is warm-blooded. A typical reptile has dry, scaly skin and is cold-blooded. That means its body temperature stays about the same temperature as its surroundings.

Reptiles lived on Earth before mammals. Mammals evolved (developed over a long time) from a group of reptiles. When dinosaurs ruled the world, there were some mammals, too. But most were small and not very important.

Baluchitherium lived during a time called the Age of Mammals. This was after the dinosaurs died out. Baluchitherium later died out, too. Its habitat turned into a desert. There were no longer trees and lush plants to eat.

Believe it or not, very early rhinos were fast runners. They had thin legs and were much smaller than Baluchitherium. The later rhinos were much bigger. They had thick, heavy legs that looked like columns. Some rhinos, like those of today, also had horns. Baluchitherium, however, did not. Do you think Baluchitherium might have needed horns for protection? Why or why not?

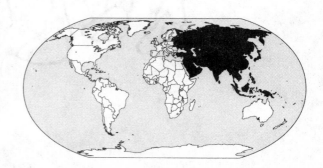

# DIATRYMA
## Tertiary Period

**Diatryma** (dy-uh-TRY-muh)

Imagine seeing a <u>bird</u> as tall as your living room ceiling! That was Diatryma in the Tertiary Period almost 50 million years ago. It towered over many mammals of that time. And it ate a good number of them. This included the ancestor of the horse, which was then about the size of a rabbit or small dog.

Diatryma had very small wings and could not fly. But this was no problem for Diatryma. It had long, powerful legs and probably ran faster than most carnivorous (kar-NIV-or-us), or meat-eating, animals. It was strong enough to kill any one of them.

Diatryma is also called the "terror crane." Besides its giant size, it also had a huge, sharp beak. It could snatch up a whole animal in a single swoop. And once it locked those jaws, its prey was history.

Then there were Diatryma's killer claws. They were like the talons that eagles have but much larger. This bird could sink these claws into an animal and rip its hide apart. Few animals wanted to tangle with the "terror crane."

The time in which Diatryma lived was called the Age of Mammals. It was after the dinosaurs died out. When the huge meat-eating dinosaurs had ruled the world, there were also many small mammals. But they had hidden from the dinosaurs. Now they could evolve (develop slowly) into larger mammals. There was also more food to eat. And these animals developed larger brains.

This was also a time when new families of animals came to be. Descendants of these animals still exist today: whales, bats, camels, horses, and elephants. Back then, though, these animals looked quite different. Some were bigger and some, like the ancestor of the horse, were much smaller than they are today.

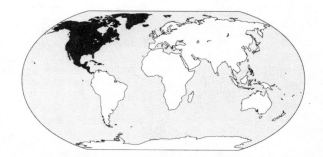

# PLATYBELODON
## Middle Tertiary Period

**Platybelodon** (plat-ee-BEL-uh-don)

Imagine what it must have been like 20 million years ago. A huge elephant–like creature was standing near the edge of a lake. It was feeding on plants that live in the water. It had the perfect mouth for scooping up its food out of the water. Its enormous lower jaw was shaped like a shovel. At the end were two flat teeth, or tusks. These teeth stuck straight out in front. As the animal moved forward through the water, it cut the plants and roots with these shovel-teeth.

The animal ate and ate. It needed lots of food to fill up its huge body. It moved farther into the lake to find more water plants. But all of a sudden, it stepped too far. The bottom of the lake dropped off. The animal began to sink into a deep hole filled with thick, gooey mud. It couldn't free itself. It panicked and thrashed around. The animal called to its "buddies" at the edge of the lake. Some of them came to help, but they too got caught in the muddy hole. About 20 huge creatures were hopelessly trapped.

This is probably what happened to a herd of animals called Platybelodon. It may have happened to many other prehistoric animals as well. Scientists think this because they have found many fossil bones of certain animals all in one place. In this case, the Platybelodons were stuck in thick mud and that's where they died. The mud later became hard, green clay. It surrounded the animals' bones.

Platybelodon is called the shovel-tusker. Its name means "flat frontal tooth." It was related to the mastodon, or hairy elephant. Platybelodon is also called the "bulldozer elephant" because of its eating habits with those shovel-teeth. It could go into a lake or pond and "mow down" its food in no time.

Platybelodon was a mammal found in Asia. It lived during a time called the Age of Mammals. By this time, the dinosaurs had died out. Large and small mammals now ruled the Earth.

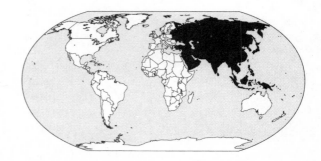

# DIPROTODON
## Late Tertiary to Early Quaternary Period

**Diprotodon** (dip-ROH-tuh-don)

Diprotodon was an early marsupial. A marsupial (mar-SOOP-ee-uhl) is an animal with a pouch. A kangaroo is an example of a marsupial. When a baby kangaroo is born, it is very tiny and not well developed. It crawls into the mother's pouch. There it stays until it is bigger and can take care of itself.

Diprotodon was a BIG marsupial. It looked somewhat like a hairy hippo with clawed feet. It was an ancestor of the wombat. A wombat is a small tail-less animal that lives in a burrow. Diprotodon, at 11 feet long, was much too big to dig a burrow, though. It probably lived near lakes or streams in order to find plants to eat.

Skeletons of Diprotodon have been found in Lake Calabonna in southeastern Australia. They were stuck in hardened mud. This is what probably happened:

It was warm for a long period of time. There was little rain. A dry, salty crust formed on the top of Lake Calabonna. Diprotodon was at the edge of the lake. It was busy munching the soft green leaves on the bushes around the lake. Thinking that the lake was dry, solid mud, it stepped onto the surface. Big mistake! Diprotodon quickly became trapped in the gooey mud. It thrashed about, but this just made it worse. The more it struggled, the deeper it sank. Soon it was under the surface, where it drowned.

This must have happened over and over to Diprotodon and other animals. Many skeletons have been found all in the same place in Lake Calabonna.

Diprotodon lived during the Age of Mammals. This was after the dinosaurs had died out. Most of the giant mammals lived during the last 38 million years. Many of them roamed the Earth until just two million years ago. This is when the first people lived here. Perhaps they hunted mammals like Diprotodon and the giant woolly elephants called mammoths.

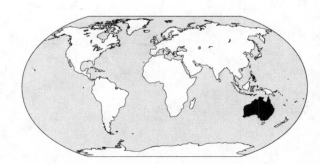

# GLYPTODON
## Late Tertiary to Early Quaternary Period

**Glyptodon** (GLIP-tuh-don)

The Time—About one million years ago
The Place—The grasslands of southern South America
The Characters—Glyptodon and a giant saber-toothed cat

It is a hot afternoon with the sun still blazing in the sky. A gentle breeze blows across the top of the long pampas grass. For a moment there is some rustling in the grass. Then it stops. All that can be seen is a big saber-toothed cat and what looks like a bumpy rock. The cat is sniffing all around the rock. He is sure that rock is alive. Hadn't it just moved? Then all of a sudden—WHUMP! The "rock" smacks the cat with the end of its bony, spiked tail. It is a good shot, too. One of the sharp spikes catches the end of the cat's nose. It rips a chunk out of it. The cat YELPS and runs away. That is probably the last time it will bother a Glyptodon.

With a bony war club for a tail and a thick shell like a turtle, it's surprising that Glyptodon became extinct. The only animal that is anything like it today is the armadillo. An armadillo's shell has bony rings. Glyptodon's shell was hard like a turtle's. Both the armadillo and the Glyptodon have hair on their bodies.

Plus, Glyptodon was much larger than today's armadillo. It was 9 to 15 feet long—maybe the length of your bedroom. And it had short, chubby, furry legs. It probably didn't move too fast. So it was a good thing it had armor on its body, a helmet on its head, and that war club for a tail.

Glyptodon probably ate insects, worms, and berries. How do scientists know this? They have looked at Glyptodon's teeth, which were like flat pegs. It couldn't have attacked other animals. It couldn't have munched on tough, woody plants and grasses of the grassland. So it probably ate soft foods that needed little or no chewing.

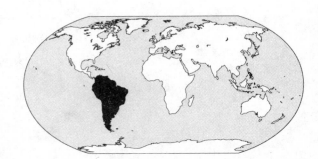

# MEGATHERIUM
## Late Tertiary to Early Quaternary Period

**Megatherium** (meg-uh-THEE-ree-um)

A sloth (SLAWTH) is a furry animal that lives in the jungles of Central and South America. It spends most of its time hanging upside down from tree branches. Its long claws wrap around tree limbs and keep it from falling. Here it feeds on leaves and buds, moving slowly from one end of a branch to the other.

This two-foot sloth is today's relative of Megatherium. Megatherium's name means "giant beast." It was truly *mega*—it was about the size of an elephant. Could you imagine this giant sloth hanging from a tree branch? It might pull the whole tree over.

Megatherium was actually a ground sloth. But it did have long, curved claws on its feet, much like today's sloth. It used these claws to dig for food and to pull tree branches to its mouth. The claws also came in handy as weapons. One swipe with this huge clawed paw could leave a bleeding wound in another animal.

Megatherium had trouble walking on its feet with those curved claws, though. So it walked on its front knuckles and the sides of its back feet. It probably waddled instead of walked. It was not a graceful sight!

Megatherium ate only plants. But it did not compete with many other animals for its food. It could stand up on its back legs and lean on its thick, strong tail. Then it was almost 20 feet tall. Few other animals were that big. It could reach the tops of tall trees. Then it used its long tongue to pull leaves off the trees.

Megatherium was a mammal that came after the dinosaurs died out. As with many other mammals, its young were born alive and lived on the mother's milk. Megatherium also had lots of thick hair all over its body. It may have needed this fur because the Earth started to get cooler during the Age of Mammals. It had been hot and steamy during most of the Age of Dinosaurs.

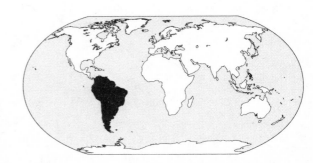